Lene

Tatted bookmarks
- cross-shaped

Akacia

Drawings: Lene Bjørn

Forlaget Akacia
Skovvænget 1
DK - 5690 Tommerup
akacia@akacia.dk

Printed at Øko-Tryk I/S, Videbæk, Denmark, 2003

ISBN: 87-7847-062-5

Introduction

I have always made different types of needlework, but because tatting is so easy to carry with you, it has become my favourite.

Many years ago when my daughter was to be confirmed, I thought I would like to tat a cross for her hymnbook. And through the years I have continued making bookmarks for the candidates for confirmation in the family and among close friends. For this book I have chosen twelve crosses, all named after the girl who received it.

I hope, that you will get as much pleasure out of these bookmarks, as I had designing them.

Happy tatting.
Lene Bjørn

Explanation of symbols

Chain

Ring

Picot = p

Split ring

Josephine knot = half knots formed into a ring

Spiral cord = half knots formed into a chain

Double knots = dk

Half double knots = hk

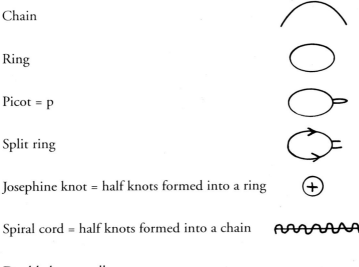

Materials

Shuttles
Crochet hook
Paper clips
A pair of scissors
Sewing needle
Starch
Crochet thread no 40.
Each cross measures roughly 7 x 9 cm. If you want a smaller cross, work
with a thinner tread; if you want a bigger cross, work with a thicker tread.

Lock stitch and false picot

A lock stitch is made of a reversed 1st half of the stitch followed by a correct 2nd half of the stitch.

A false picot is created when you omit to tighten the 1st half of the stitch completely.

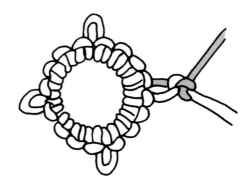

Picot on spiral

12 right half knots, space 1 left half knots (=picot), 12 right half knots, pull the chain tight and twist it 4 times.

Heidi

1 shuttle.
The cross is tatted in one round.
The chains are made of Josephine
knots with 8 half knots in each
ring.

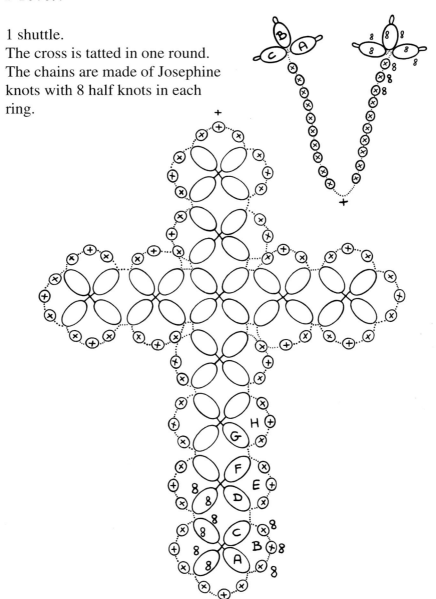

Maria

1 shuttle + ball thread.
The cross is tatted i one round.

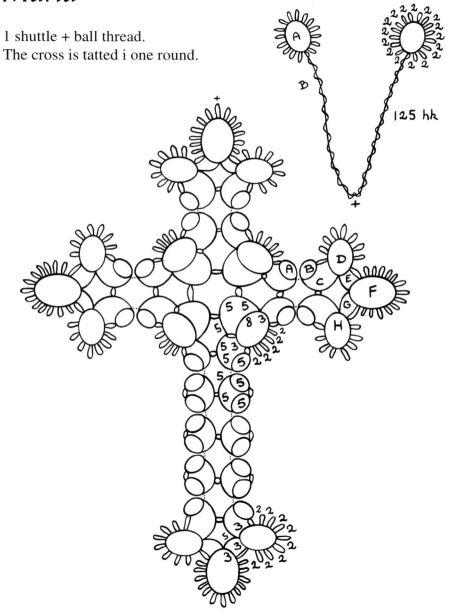

125 hk

Christina

1 shuttle + ball thread.
The cross is tatted in one round.

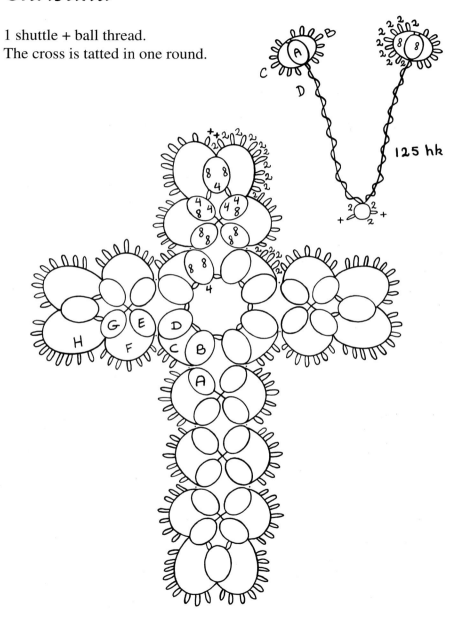

125 hk

Helene

1 shuttle + ball thread.
The cross is tatted in one round.
All chains are spirals made of
half knots (see page 5).

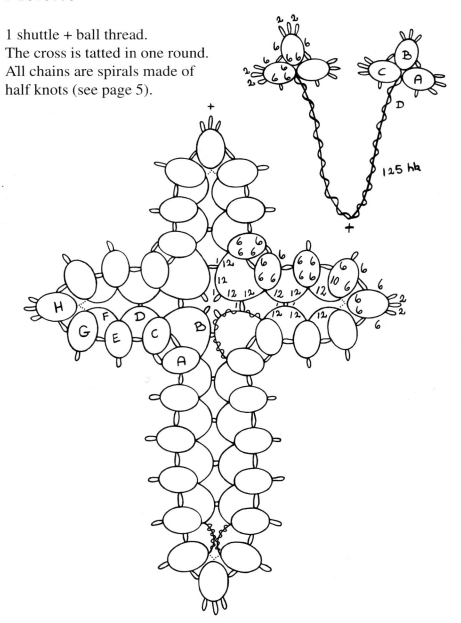

125 hk

13

Regina

2 shuttles.
The cross is made in two rounds.
Start making the center motiv
from A to E. Second round starts
with F.

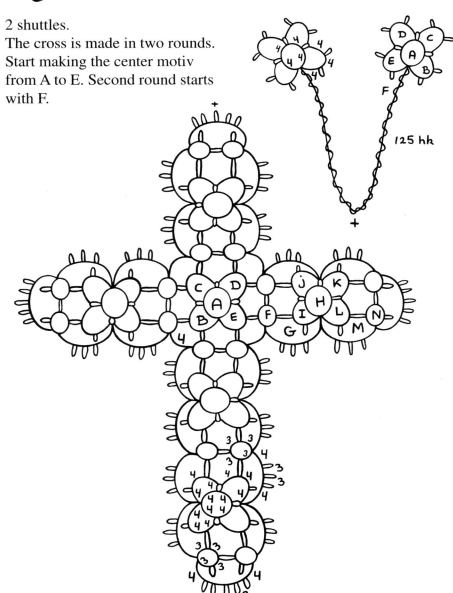

125 hh

Heidi   *Maria*   *Christina*

Helene   *Regina*   *Laura*

Monica   Pernille   Malene

Camilla   Amalie   Katrine

Laura

1 shuttle + ball thread.
Each flower is tatted seperately and
joined together according to the diagram.
The last picot in the center ring is a false
picot (see page 5); continue with chains
without breaking the thread.

125 hl

Monica

2 shuttles.
The cross is tatted in one round.

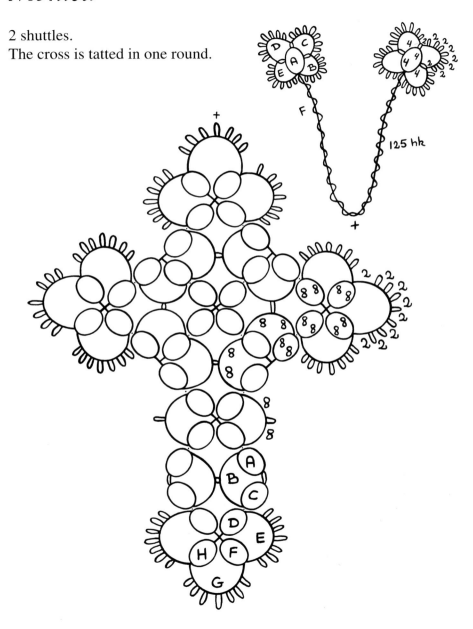

Pernille

2 shuttles.
The cross is tatted in one round.

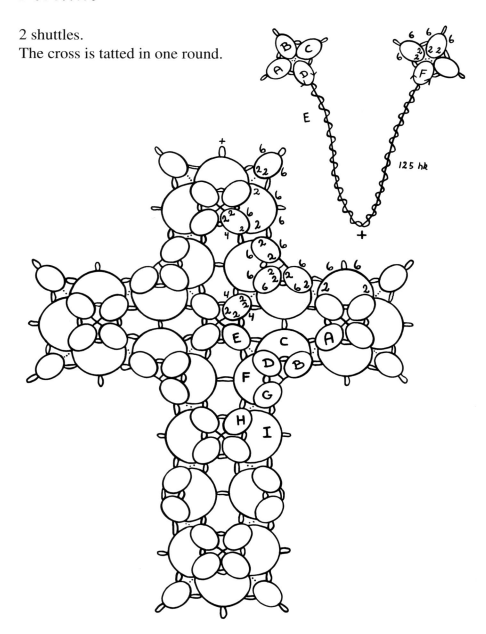

Malene

2 shuttles.
The cross is tatted in one round.
A (heart) = ring.

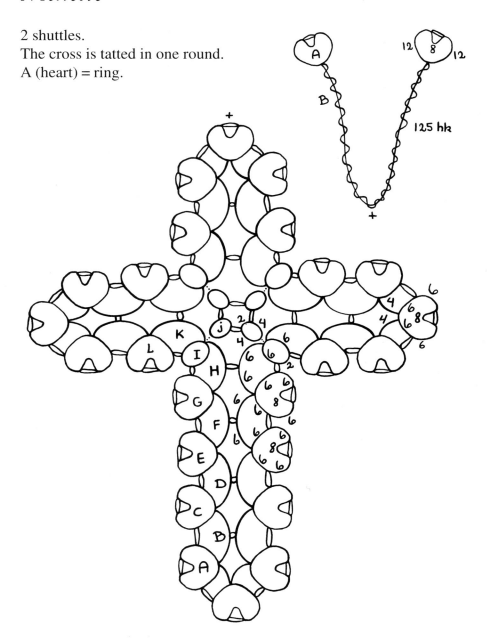

Camilla

2 shuttles.
The cross is tatted in one round.

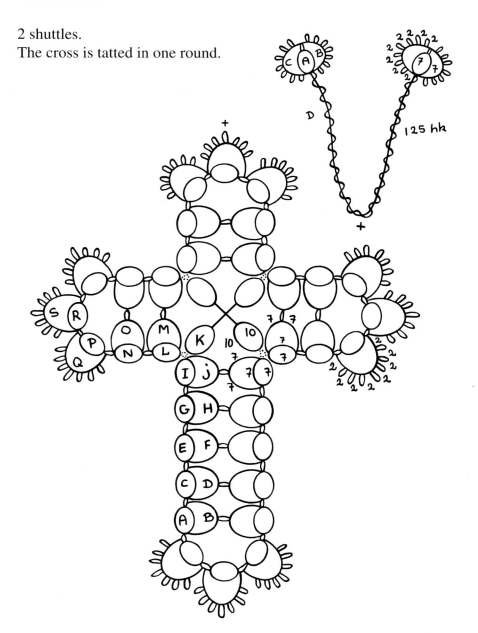

Amalie

2 shuttles.
3 paper clips.
The cross is tatted in one round.
Start with a paper clip in A,
because it is a chain.

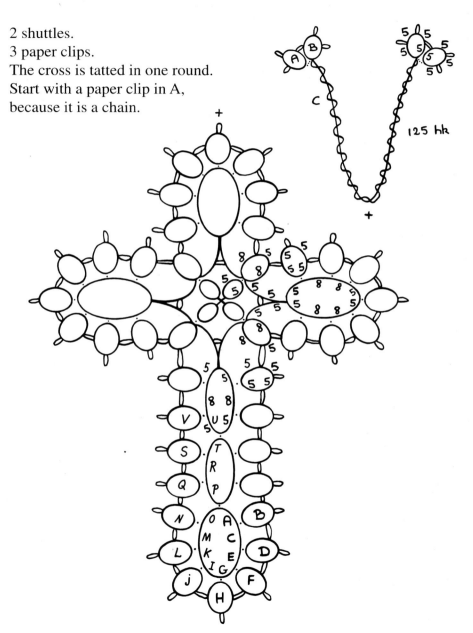

125 hk

Katrine

2 shuttles.
The cross is tatted in one round.
The outmost row consists of
joined rings.

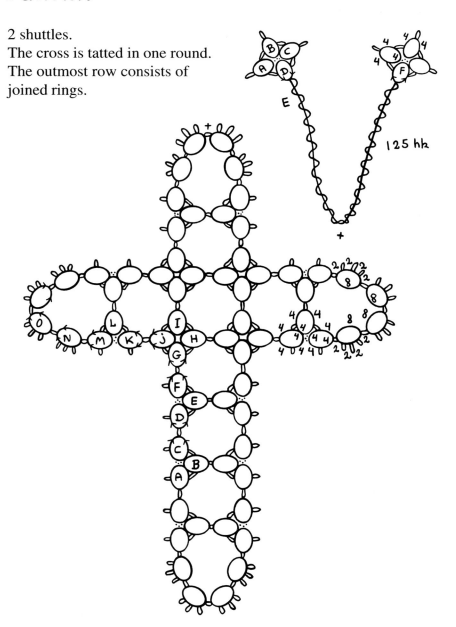

125 hk